INTERMEDIATE SNARE DRUM STUDIES

By

Mitchell Peters

Exclusive Distributor:

PROFESSIONAL DRUM SHOP, INC.
854 Vine Street,
Hollywood, California — U.S.A.

Published by

TRY PUBLISHING COMPANY
Hollywood, California — U.S.A.

Copyright© 1976 by Mitchell Peters
Copyright© Assigned 2009 to TRY PUBLISHING COMPANY, Hollywood, California — U.S.A.

1

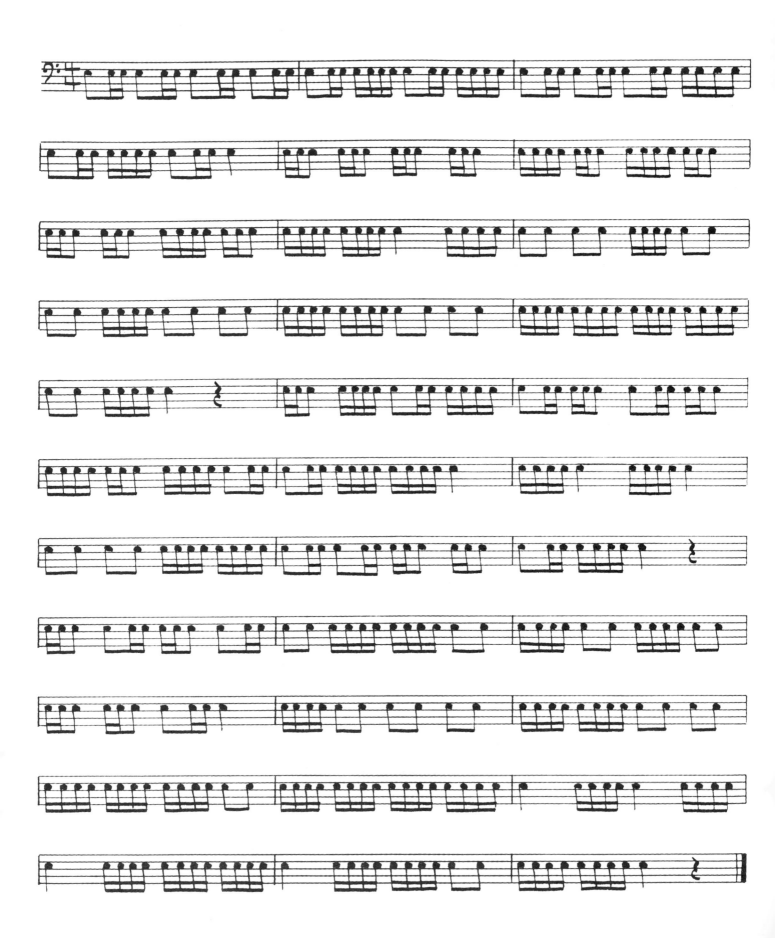

II

III

IV

V

THE THREE CAMPS (A Traditional Drum Solo) 3 Hand Motions Per Pulse

VI

THE THREE CAMPS - VARIATION I - 4 Hand Motions Per Pulse

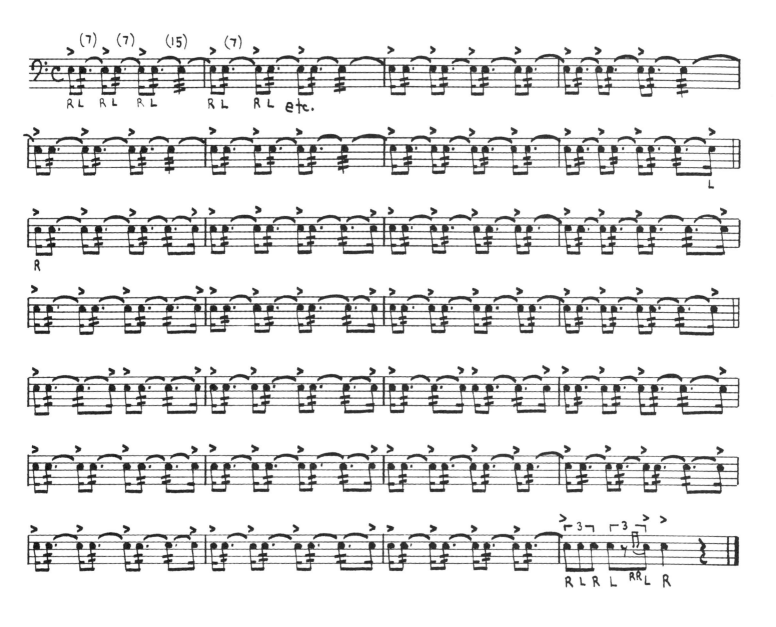

VII

THE THREE CAMPS - VARIATION II - 5 Hand Motions Per Pulse

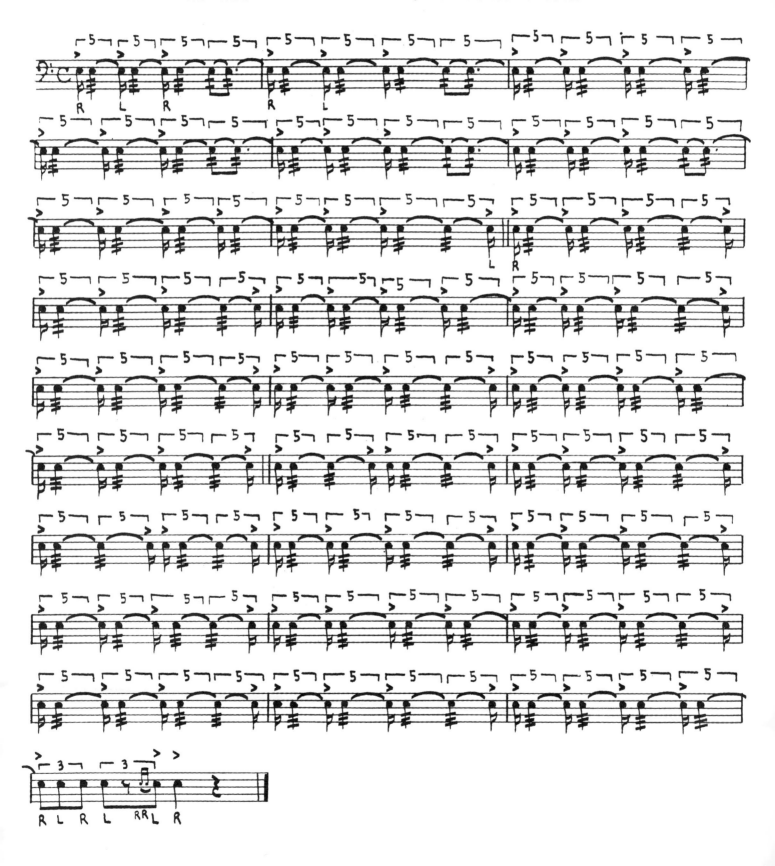

VIII

THE THREE CAMPS - VARIATION III - 6 Hand Motions Per Pulse

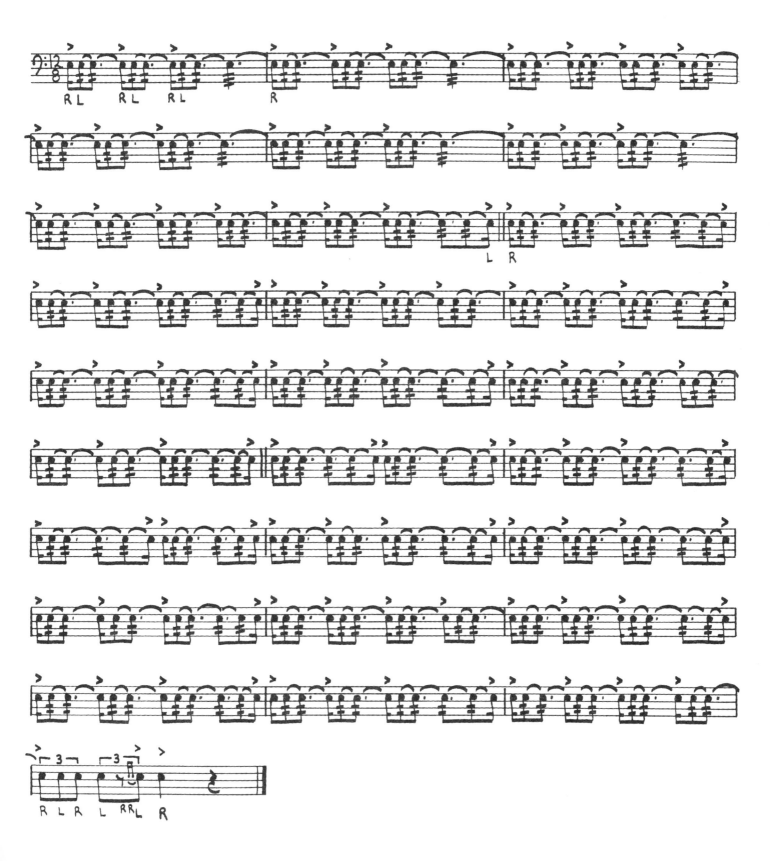

IX

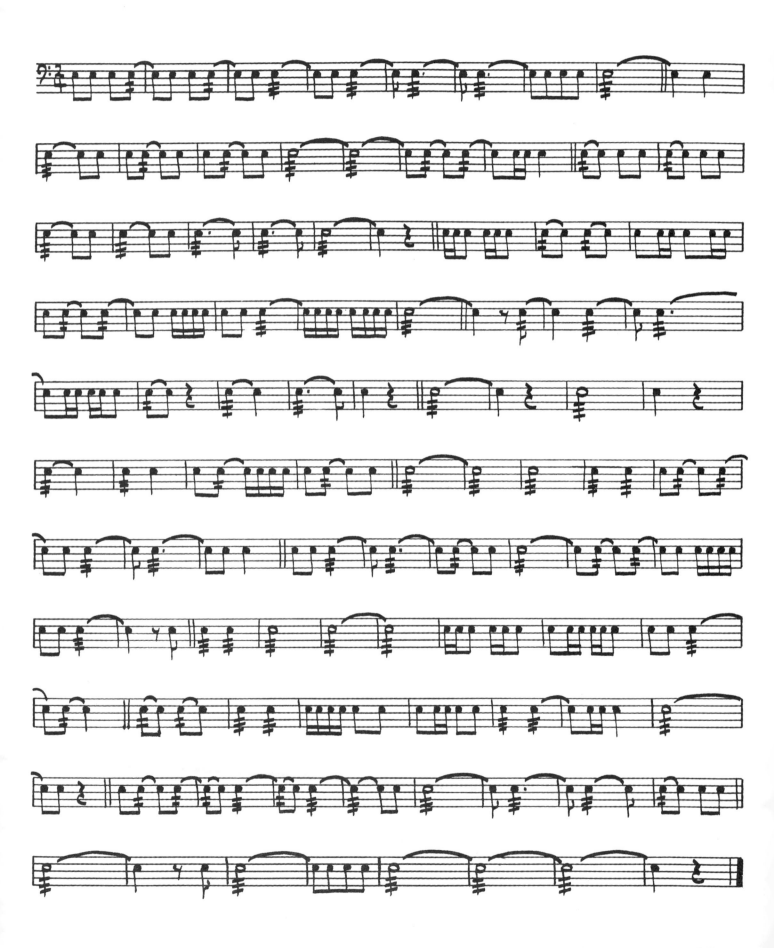

X

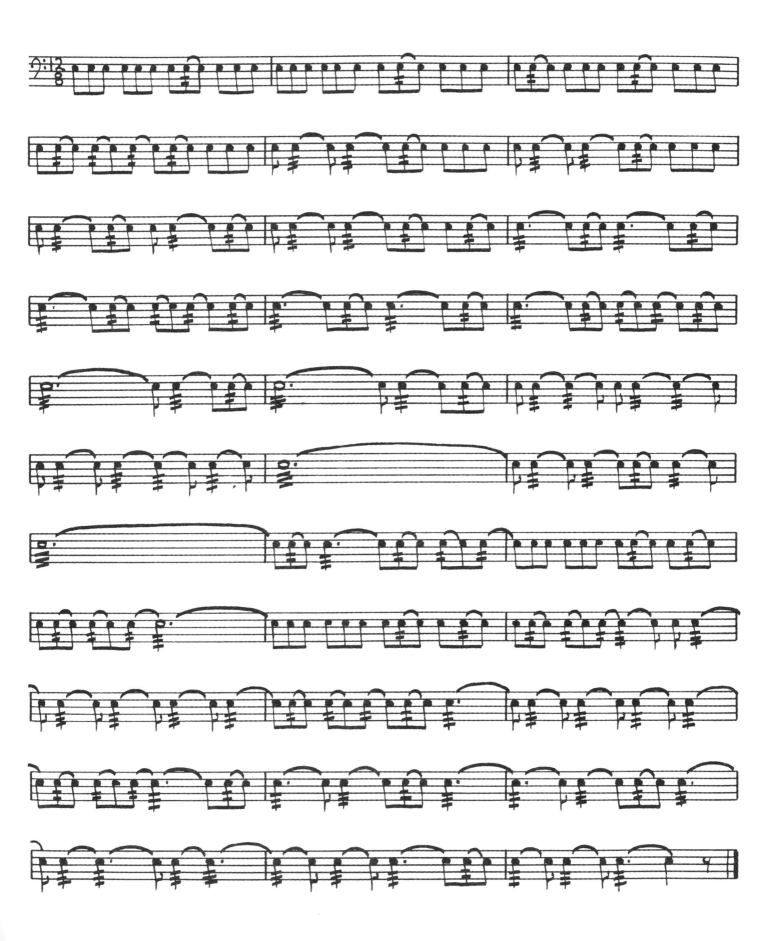

XI

FOR PRACTICE, IN THE ABOVE STUDY PLAY RUFFS IN PLACE OF THE FLAMS

1

3

5

8

9

14

16

17

18

19

20

21

22

23

24

26

27

28

29

31

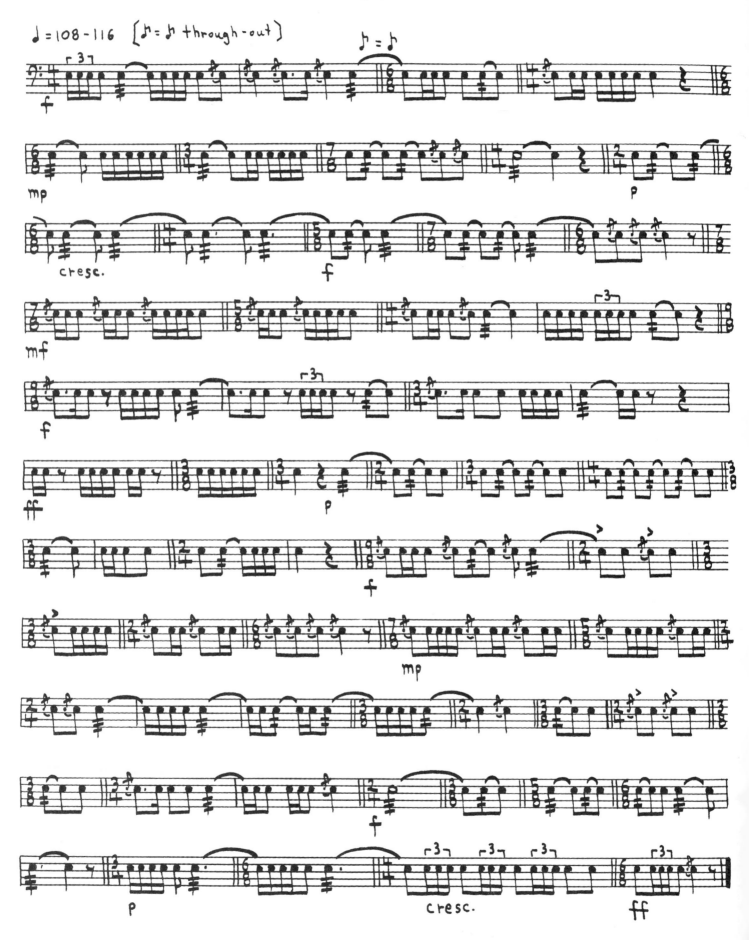